LONDON

PASSING · FACES

LONDON

PASSING · FACES

Michael Dowty

ALAN SUTTON

ALAN SUTTON PUBLISHING
BRUNSWICK ROAD · GLOUCESTER

ALAN SUTTON PUBLISHING INC
WOLFEBORO FALLS · NEW HAMPSHIRE
NH 03896-0848

First published in the United Kingdom in 1989
First published in the United States of America in 1990

British Library Cataloguing in Publication Data

Dowty, Michael
London: Passing Faces.
1. London, 1945-
I. Title
942.1085
ISBN 0-86299-679-1

Library of Congress Cataloging in Publication Data
applied for

Typesetting and origination by
Alan Sutton Publishing Limited
Printed in Great Britain by
WBC Print Limited

INTRODUCTION

It's funny how certain things stick in the mind and refuse to go away. I have been haunted for years by a radio sketch in which a book-borrower presented his selection of wildly varied titles for date-stamping at the library counter, only to fall victim to a bitter verbal attack from the librarian. Utterly bewildered, the borrower enquired what was wrong with his choice: 'Oh, there's nothing wrong,' replied the librarian, with a sort of controlled savagery, 'you've just got a grasshopper mind, that's all. Can't concentrate on anything for more than a few minutes at a time!'

Such a sketch was bound to speak volumes to one whose shelves had long held all sorts and conditions of books and magazines, designed to be flipped through rather than read. By coincidence I recently blew the dust from an old *Lilliput*, dated July 1949, and found an advertisement for Pelmanism: 'You know the man with a "Grasshopper Mind" as well as you know yourself. His mind nibbles at everything and masters nothing.' Further graphic illustration of this distressing malady was followed by promise of a cure — enrolment with the Pelman Institute would banish mind-wandering, inferiority and indecision, and replace them with concentration, optimism and reliability.

Had I only taken note of the advertisement at the time of its publication, my life might have been transformed. I could certainly have done with a dose of Pelmanism to see me through my first London encounter in 1950 when, aged twenty, overawed and acutely embarrassed by the deadly formality of the hotel into which I had booked, I crept out, unobserved and breakfastless, to sit a photographic examination on a severely empty stomach. The examination was cheerfully and expectedly failed, and I went home to Worcester with my first two London photographs (pages 2 and 3) as sole salvage from a wretched experience. The other reproductions in this book bear witness to my survival, and a willingness to risk subsequent visits to London, and even to live there for several years.

Understandably enough, I rather wanted the title to be *Grasshopper's London*, on account of the erratic, jumping-around nature of the contents. My publisher, however, gently, reasonably and rightly hopped me down a less frivolous path, for here are close on thirty years of faces (not necessarily human), fleetingly passing the camera and providing glimpses of what is otherwise irrevocably changed or lost to us for ever.

The photographs are broadly in chronological order, and with few exceptions are dated. The bulk of them are from what I will grandly call my 'residential periods', firstly in the late fifties as a single man, then as a married one in the early sixties, when Elizabeth and I moved rapidly from Birmingham after three weeks of marriage (no one was chasing us, and we had paid the rent), to be told by an ethereal girl at the flat agency: 'You can't just expect to come to London and move straight into a flat.' We moved into the first one

we viewed. It was genuinely spacious, well decorated and equipped, situated above a chemist's, flanked by other shops and just around the corner from West Hampstead underground station which, being overground, made it possible for either of us to spot the other alighting at the platform and to get the kettle boiled. For all these Broadhurst Gardens benefits we paid six guineas a week in 1960.

We made the most of our time there, going to concerts at the Festival Hall and free ones at BBC Maida Vale Studios. We visited the museums and art galleries, and went to the theatre for *West Side Story, Beyond The Fringe, Billy Liar* and *Stop the World, I Want to Get Off*, to name but four. We even took Elizabeth's parents to see *The Mousetrap* – and regretted it. We all regretted it! And somewhere in the middle of all this London life came our first holiday, in Scotland, the return from which was almost immediately marred by the theft of the wheel-trims from our elderly Beetle. My reporting of the fact at West Hampstead police station was unsympathetically received by the desk sergeant: 'You're lucky. One of our detectives had his car stolen from outside the station.'

Even harsher facts of London life were revealed to us when we ventured into expectant parenthood and rapidly discovered the 'no room at the inn' mentality (which, of course, is universal). Luckily for us, we were given shelter at Highgate by a good friend, Richard Thornbury, long before the baby was due. It was from there, at 4.30 on a sunny May Saturday morning, that I drove Elizabeth past a bird-song-filled Hampstead Heath to Queen Mary's Maternity Home, where we parted company, being dreadfully unenlightened and

more enthusiastic about sharing the product than the process.

Faced with the problem of how to pass the anxious hours, I was fortuitously presented with what seemed to be the perfect solution: Middlesex were at home to our own native county, and what better balm could there be than three bob's worth of Lord's and the Worcestershire batsmen enjoying themselves in the sunshine? Alas! it was all an idle dream, for when I got to the ground, fifteen minutes after play had commenced, Worcestershire were 6 for 1 and though the sun did shine, it shone for Middlesex. A boundary by Devereux from the penultimate ball before lunch took the score to 46 for 6, and the only entertainment (unless you were a Middlesex supporter) had been provided by the Lord's cat making two unsuccessful sorties from the pavilion in hilariously vain pursuit of birds. That's the trouble with cricket, it never goes according to plan, and the laughs keep coming in the wrong places. I vacated my seat and left the ground.

Fiona, by the way, was born very late on the same day, at two minutes to midnight on the last day of National Nature Week in National Productivity Year. She refused to look at me until the following Thursday, and with a set of credentials like those, I'm not altogether surprised.

Whether or not any of this has been of the slightest interest to you I have no way of knowing, but it has certainly helped me out of a hole, for how else could I have introduced my own impressions of London, without falling short of my own mind-wandering standards? I'm still an old-fashioned grasshopper at heart.

Michael Dowty
1989

Passing Faces

An immense, slow-flowing queue of humanity (inching towards the entrance to the Pompeii Exhibition at the Royal Academy in February 1977).

Trafalgar Square

Summer 1950

Almost forty years on, it has lost much of its leisurely atmosphere, but for many
visitors will always remain London's focal point and the place to go if you want to
study humanity without expending too much energy.

Broadcasting House and All Souls church
Summer 1950

High on the BBC's solid, dependable façade, the clock stands at noon and all is well. Even the bomb-damaged All Souls is being restored. But these were innocent days, before the cold-blooded murder of Children's Hour, the sudden disappearance of Kenneth Robinson and the threatened axing of ball-by-ball cricket commentaries.

Festival of Britain
1951

The South Bank Exhibition's Dome of Discovery and Skylon, viewed from
Victoria Embankment across the Thames.

4

South Bank Exhibition

Looking out from beneath the eaves of the dome to the Sea and Ships Pavilions
and the fountains. In the right foreground is John Cobb's Railton Special with
which he held the world's land speed record.

Inside the Dome

Even without the exhibits it was a wonderfully uplifting experience just to stand
inside this vast creation whose maximum diameter was 365 ft – big enough, we
were told, to provide umbrella cover for the whole of Trafalgar Square.

British Discovery and Exploration

These were the display themes within the dome, dominated by one of the six largest telescopes in the world. It was on loan for the exhibition before shipment to the Australian Commonwealth Observatory at Mount Stromlo, near Canberra.

Awe-Inspiring concept
July 1952

Rowland Emett was hardly likely to be outshone by a mere star-gazing telescope, and he duly displayed the product of his supreme vision at the Festival Pleasure Gardens, Battersea. The rails of Evercreech Junction had been left far behind by this ultimate achievement in the field of transport, capable of plumbing the ocean depths and attaining stratospheric heights – and all stations in between, simultaneously, maybe. No disrespect to Emett's genius is intended by recording the little matter of the English Electric Canberra's crossing the Atlantic in 3 hours 25 minutes, the following month.

Sign here, please
July 1952

This gentleman was, I believe, a long-distance lorry driver. He used to frequent the *Prospect of Whitby* at Wapping, hence his nickname: Prospect Jock. He wore his strange hobby for all to see, for it consisted of collecting autographs on his hat, shirt and tie. I seem to recall being told that Princess Margaret's name was there, somewhere. The entranced-looking lady in the background is actually my sister who married the man so honourably mentioned on page 18.

Running out of track

1 July 1953

A month after the Queen's Coronation, London's trams came to an end. This one,
on the Victoria Embankment at Charing Cross Pier, is a No. 40, heading for
Kennington.

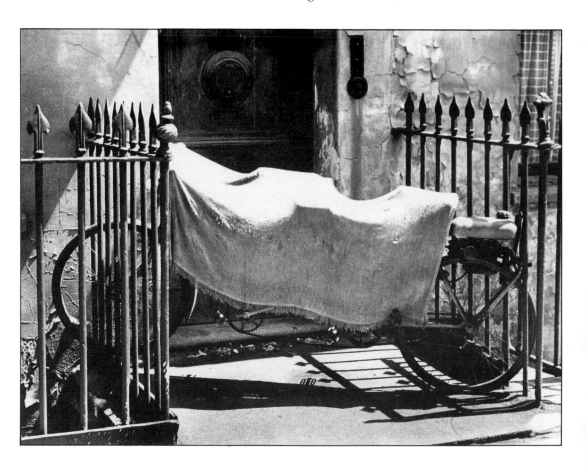

Parked between the railings
1 July 1953

A quite novel solution to the problem of tandem-storage. It raises the tiny
question of access to the house, but no doubt the owners had their methods.

Reclining figure

On an unknown date, back in the 1950s when the modest admission charge of
3*d*. enabled visitors to Kew Gardens to spend a day improving their botanical
knowledge or shutting out all knowledge of anything. And in those days, one's
peace suffered less frequently from the excesses of Heathrow.

Inclining bear
1 July 1953

Mischa, husband of Ivy and father of the famous Brumas, holding sway over his public at Regent's Park. For a time, attention was critically focused on this enclosure, to the dismay of lesser bears bemoaning the sudden decline in the bun market as they skulked about their dens of Kodiak camera obscurity.

13

Coronation arches

A month after the event, the arches remained to dominate the Mall. There were four of them spanning the carriageway and rising to a height of roughly 65 ft, surmounted by 20 ft lions and unicorns.

Tower Bridge

A view from the pier.

Power Bridge

Battersea Power Station from Chelsea Bridge.

The Duellists: water pistols for two

2 August 1955

Whilst this might appear less than apt phraseology, it would have appealed to an anonymous critic of Trafalgar Square in the 19th century who dismissed it as: 'A dreary waste of asphalt with two squirts.' How difficult it is to please everyone with one's best endeavours. Happily, on the credit side, Sir Robert Peel thought it: 'The finest site in Europe', although I am not at all sure if he was referring purely to the site or the finished scheme which was spread over a large number of years . . .

. . . Work commenced in 1829, but Landseer's lions were not installed until 1867, whilst Nelson's Column apparently took from 1840 to 1849 to construct. A story concerning the statue itself tells of an official involved with the project who, tiring of being constantly asked how Nelson got on top of the column, took to replying: 'We put a springboard in the square, Nelson took a running jump and just managed to get there.'

Two Ladies of Lisle Street

Photographed on 22 February 1958, this duo had been briefly encountered on the previous day when my brother-in-law Ralph Jones and I walked past and received a most charming verbal invitation on a chilly afternoon: 'Would you like to come inside?' Ralph, a native of south Wales and never known to be anything less than perfectly mannered, softly replied, without slackening pace: 'Oh, no thank you. We're just going to have our tea.' I resolved, there and then, to return the following day and attempt a photograph of the kindly pair. It was again chilly, dark, and snow was falling as I focused under cover of a temporarily stranded van. Having released the shutter, I walked swiftly up the street with voices calling after me and the expectation of a knife between the shoulder-blades.

Underground exhaustion
22 August 1958

Doorstep doubts
20 July 1959

From rags to rags

20 July 1959

Totting-up the day's tally.

Street trading

27 July 1959

We are a broad-based company, dealing in consumer usables and thoroughly
customer-orientated.

The Houses of Parliament

Where you can be up in the air one minute, and flat on your face the next.

The trampoline

12 August 1959

Where you can be up in the air one minute, and flat on your face the next.

A solitude of nun
5 August 1959

A weave of baskets
5 August 1959

A muscularity of Mackeson

5 August 1959

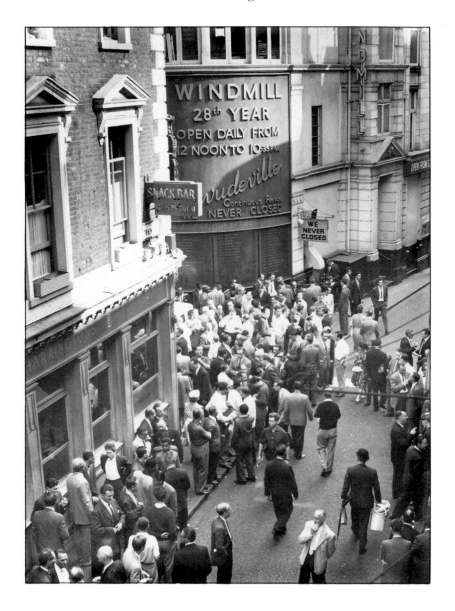

A loiter of musicians
7 September 1959

They were generally known as 'The Archer Street Mob', and stood around on
Mondays, hoping for work. Behind them, the Windmill Theatre had been
steadily employed for nearly twenty-eight years.

Moving in

7 September 1959

Smith's Court, W1.

Stepping out
7 September 1959

Ambling along
7 September 1959
Great Windmill Street.

Taking it easy
19 September 1959

... Where the ease is taken

The leisurely pipe-smoker occupies the corner of Emmett Street, watching his
Saturday morning world go by at the junction with Bridge Road, close to West
India Dock. Should he feel like a bit of a read, there are still three copies of the
News Chronicle in the newsagent's rack, with the banner headline – literally –
'BAN ALL ARMS BY 1963. MR K.' My word, wasn't he ambitious?

Brick, faced

19 September 1959

A Docklands answer to Hampstead's annual open-air art exhibition.

Wall-backed

19 September 1959

Boy meets girls.

We've been framed
19 September 1959

We're barred
19 September 1959

Poplar Boys
19 September 1959

Poplar girl
19 September 1959

Orderly retreat
19 September 1959

United front
19 September 1959

Massed protest

20 September 1959

They're all marching on Mr K.'s side.

Friendly persuasion

Rattling box and open purse, in aid of the cause.

Leisurely law

Nothing much to report at the moment.

Active order

28 September 1959

A little after 9 a.m., and how gently the officers help the man to cross Piccadilly
Circus. He's a little upset about something – you can see that from the
stress-marks on his jacket. I once used this as a Christmas card; it wasn't very
seasonal, but at least it was quite arresting.

Foggy pots

6 November 1959

Haverstock Hill. Clean air hadn't yet filtered through to de-smog London. In the absence of smoke from these chimneys the fires must have been lit elsewhere. Or was the fog a hangover from the previous night's activities?

Cart-pulling
16 November 1959

Fruit-pushing
16 November 1959

'Goodness, how you startled me!'
20 July 1959

Arthur Hutt and George

7 August 1960

What's his line?

The answer is John Line & Sons Ltd., the Tottenham Court Road suppliers (Royal Warrant) of paints and wallpapers. Mr Hutt had been delivering for them for fifteen years, together with pale grey George. 'Titch', as all 5ft 2in of him was known, obligingly posed by the van in St Giles High Street and gleefully imparted little-known facts on the advantages of being horse-drawn in London traffic, before driving off into – what else? – a long line of it. He and George retired in October 1962.

Public worship

23 October 1960

Prayers in Hyde Park.

Private thoughts

2 November 1960

Almost screened by a tree, a lonely figure sits hunched amongst Hyde Park's
autumn leaves.

Newsboy?

5 November 1960

Not exactly. He's actually collecting combustibles for an annual conflagration.

Precarious summit

5 November 1960

Nine boys building a bonfire. One has reached ambition's peak, others are negotiating upper slopes, whilst the remainder potter about the foothills and base camp.

Firm base

6 November 1960

Well-heeled spectators at the feet of Achilles, awaiting the start of another
popular annual event – the RAC's London to Brighton Veteran Car Run.

Anxious anticipation

6 November 1960

Keyed-up participants at Hyde Park, awaiting the 8 a.m. start.

Dignified departure

6 November 1960

Sedately setting out from Serpentine Road, this Malvernia, dating from 1898, was the only known surviving model from the firm of C. Santler & Co. Ltd., of Malvern Link, Worcestershire.

Helmets

13 November 1960

Caps

11 December 1960

Cheerfully itinerant

The merry band of musicians, The Happy Wanderers, sending sounds of
pre-Christmas joy up and down the length of Petticoat Lane. And if you have ever
heard of 'trumpeter's lip', then please extend your sympathy to this obvious
sufferer from trombonist's ear. The concealed player behind him is snugly
wrapped in his sousaphone whose bell sucks the listeners into its vortex.

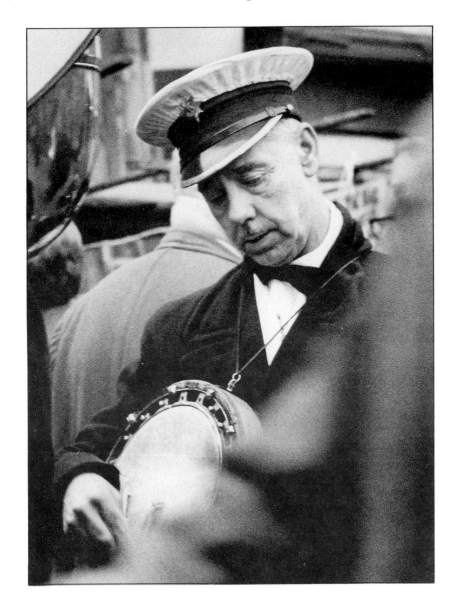

String along

Playing on the old banjo, bringing up the rear and in danger of being crowded out.

Paper song

Almost thirty years later I can still hear the voice singing out: 'Kerrier begs. Git
yer kerrier begs!'

'He's having us on!'

Doubting every word of some trader's Petticoat Lane spiel, but enjoying it.

'He's got me worried'
11 December 1960

Don't know what to think – could he be right?

Right of reply

14 January 1961

Good to find a vertical platform from which to express ourselves, before the
bulldozers move in and knock us flat.

No one to talk to
14 January 1961
He's waiting for a friend at the fringes of Covent Garden.

I tell the time

14 January 1961

St Stephen's Clock Tower, better known as the home of Big Ben which sonorously celebrated its centenary in April 1958. The old bell was sounding the eleventh hour as this photograph was taken from Westminster subway.

I speak your wait

14 January 1961

An interesting case for Harley Street, where this emaciated creature with the pinched features strikes doubt and terror into the ailing hearts of those arriving on anything more lethal than a bicycle. How thinly he stands his ground, attracting the acid comment of man, and – like his neighbour, lamp-post – the acid content of dog.

Horseguard

21 January 1961

Who guards the horse? Don't be facetious; someone has to have his head and shoulders stuck out in the rain.

Grand National?
21 January 1961

Cherry blossom

21 January 1960

Acquiring a little pedestrian polish in the Strand.

Bare branches

21 January 1961

Providing scant cover for lordly columnist.

St Paul's

22 January 1961

A distant symbol of eternity, and not a living soul in sight.

St Pancras

11 February 1961

The tree of life, and definitely no further comment.

The eyeless needle
21 January 1961

Blind justice

22 January 1961

She's beyond the reach of most of us, and the scales are almost covering her eyes.

Boys brawl in Broadhurst Gardens!
18 February 1961

Residents and passers-by attempted unsuccessfully to intervene . . .

. . . The cat from the grocer's up the road was unable to comment, partly through lack of interest, but mainly on account of the shop window being too dirty to see through.

Man of peace

18 February 1961

Bertrand Russell on the non-violent rampage again, with a lot of sit-down support. All very passive and different from the following year's Dalston episode, when Oswald Mosley and his supporters suffered from Jewish ex-servicemen who had infiltrated their meeting. *Private Eye* (long may it be able to continue paying the fines) depicted a floored Mosley on its cover for 10 August 1962, grappling with antagonists and crying, 'Bloody Fascists!' – none of which has much connection with these pictures, but I just thought you'd like to know!

'Ere we go, 'ere we go, 'ere we go . . .
17 April 1961

But not here, we don't. Camden Town.

Let's hope we don't have to
5 March 1961

Prohibition

29 April 1961

Something's happening here. We've always been able to drive this way into town,
before now.

Is it a cover-up?
29 April 1961

Actually, it's partly that, but the wraps are also coming off in readiness for the new traffic craze about to sweep the city and catch on over the whole country. It's called 'Gyratory Flow', and it's going to wreak havoc and revolutionize jam-making. Tottenham Court Road.

Up and down

7 May 1961

This is the real way to travel (as a certain Toad once, more-or-less, said). No destination to worry about, no risk of being carved-up, no fumes and no bad temper. Keep pulling the rope (wonderful training for campanologists) and enjoyably getting nowhere for ever. Richmond Park.

Round and round
7 May 1961

Four folks here with a small problem. Any idea what it might be? No, they're not lost; they know precisely where they are, and that's the problem. They're at the centre of Hampton Court Maze, wondering how on earth they're supposed to get out!

Regal team

9 May 1961

One of the Whitbread pairs drawn up by the Victoria Embankment entrance to Charing Cross underground station. Of course, that most enigmatic and anagrammatic composer, Elgar, had a preference for lager (or perhaps it was perry, but never mind), so could there be a connection between the possible fact and the naming of 'Pomp' (nearside) and 'Circumstance' (offside), resting briefly with their large load in the glare of the sun?

Cleanliness is next to? . . .

25 June 1961

It's the cat from the scruffy grocer's again. The window was still mucky, so I photographed him through the letter box. It was Sunday and peaceful, and before long – being fastidious – he settled down to wash certain parts of his anatomy. Now, we mightn't think too highly of this, but for him the counter-claim would have been: 'Cleanliness is next to the cash register.'

The eagle has landed
30 June 1961

Being Grosvenor Square, it ought to be an American one inoculated into the arm; not that it has any bearing on the story, any more than Yuri Gagarin (first man in space, in April), or Gherman Titov who didn't land his 'Eagle' until August, and certainly not Eddie Edwards who hadn't been invented at the time.
Now read on . . .

The sparrow has crashed

I know it's a let-down, but the truth sometimes is. The cocky little idiot misread
his instruments, blew the flight and came down smack in the drink . . .

. . . Fortunately, the AFR (Air Fountain Rescue) were on hand to fish him out and give him succour, which is what they turned out to be (a bunch of suckers), because the ungrateful little chap edged away from them as he dried out, then flew off without even offering the claw of friendship. If that's an example of gratitude, you can keep it!

Striding to the station
25 June 1961
West Hampstead.

Shuffling on the Heath
25 July 1961
Tramp at Hampstead.

Rooted to the ground
30 June 1961
Near Grosvenor Square.

Returned from space

17 July 1961

Following his pioneer space flight on 12 April, Major Yuri Gagarin made a
goodwill visit to this country. Here, he is seen arriving at Heathrow to catch the
plane back to Russia. It was intended to be a frontal view, but the 'Twickenham
syndrome' thwarted the intention. This particular frustration comes about when
the man in the front row of the stand jumps to his feet to see the try – and so does
everyone else. The equivalent thing occurs with pavement-lining crowds rushing
on to the carriageway and blocking the view.

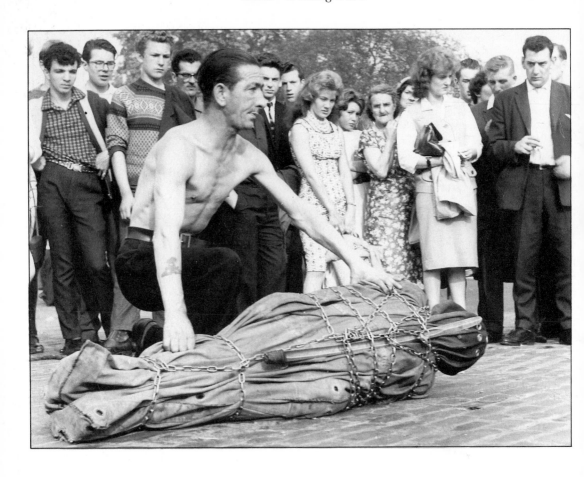

Late at the office

August 1961

Legitimate excuse No. 1. 'Sorry, Darling. Can't possibly get free for quite a time
yet.' Escapologist on Tower Hill.

Late at the office
August 1961

Legitimate excuse No. 2. 'Sorry, my dear, but I have to address this most important meeting.' Preaching to the unconvertible at Charing Cross.

THE NEW AND LATTER
HOUS...   RAEL

Extracts from the Flying Roll

God's Last Message to Man.

Speakers' Corner

Speaker cornered

August 1961

Hyde Park Corner.

If only I had wings

At 2 p.m. on Sunday 5 August 1961, a splendidly silly accident took place a short distance from Aldgate Station. Two cars were travelling west, when the one in the outside lane decided to turn left, which proved unfortunate for both owners. As it happened, a police car was passing in the opposite direction at the moment of impact, and in no time at all had screeched to a halt and discharged a small contingent of officers with notebooks at the ready, pencils licked and tape-measures flying. A stirring, reassuring sight to behold.

'Now, sir. May I see your driving licence?'

Donkey work
25 July 1961

Lightening time

Unloading shipping at London Docks.

Lighting-up time

Summer 1961

No current travel plans
1 January 1962

The Rolls with dream topping decided to see the New Year in at home.

Shooting off in all directions
1 January 1962
For the Hampstead Heath skiers and tobogganers it was a dreamily topping start
to the year.

Shot down

22 March 1962

The Shot Tower, one of London's best-loved landmarks, finally disappeared from
South Bank. Production of shot had ceased there in 1949. There was something
incongruous about having to use such a large construction for the manufacture of
a minute product. In this view, preliminary demolition work is already
underway.

Old and new faces
22 March 1962

Immediately behind the Shot Tower stands the Royal Festival Hall, with the
twenty-six storey Shell building away in the distance – rising to 351 ft above
street level.

Good luck from Queenie

And good luck to her, too, as a decent, honest, civilized representative of the
canine race. I bet her owner was a nice man, too, only I forgot to look at him. He
could have been playing a barrel-organ, a wind-up gramophone or a Jew's harp,
for all I know. The photograph was taken at Swiss Cottage, in the early 1960s.

Perhaps they need some

Two map-studying ladies, lost in Portman Square.

Chair menders

17 October 1962

What more can I add, knowing nothing of the craft or those who practise it.
South Audley Street.

Open-air sandwich

3 December 1962

A familiar figure, often seen during our West End lunch hours as he paraded his
sandwich-boards in the Selfridge's region.

Closed for lunch

2 November 1973

Here he is again, spotted during a London visit, eleven years later. For once, he
was taking it easy and talking to a blind lady with her guide dog.

Skintessential sign
28 March 1963

Could you pawn your plastic card there today, and how much might they offer
you?

Spring in Regent's Park

April 1963

This is what life ought to be for a small girl: a simple matter of being in the
sunshine at the water's edge, feeding ducks, geese and pigeons, and nothing else
mattering in the whole wide world.

Duck out of luck
April 1963

Smoke in square

17 October 1964

The square would have been either Euston or Tavistock, both of which were
minutes' walking time from Euston station.

Ever decreasing circles

17 October 1964

Idle platform trolleys at Euston. A tranquil little scene. No fuss, no bother.

Post ever so early for Christmas
18 October 1964

Here we see one of the effects of Beeching's pillage: fewer stations, greater concentration of parcels, less space for passengers. Leaving behind these mundanities, a lovely thrill of horror cruised up and down my spine when I realized I had taken this photograph of platform 1 at King's Cross from the same footbridge used by the sinister Professor Marcus when planning the robbery in *The Ladykillers*, back in 1955. Eventually thwarted by Mrs Wilberforce then, I doubt if he would have had room to evolve any kind of a plan during the rail chaos of the '60s.

Banger

18 October 1964

An abandoned wreck in Marchmont Street, near Russell Square. The street itself
looked pretty abandoned.

Bang bang
23 December 1968
Christmas window display in Regent Street.

Omnibus

27 August 1969

At the British Museum of Transport, Clapham.

Stationary monument

27 August 1969

Mallard, the world's fastest steam locomotive, reached 126 mph south of Grantham in 1938. It was brought to the Transport Museum from Nine Elms Depot on 1 March 1964, and has since been moved to the National Rail Museum at York.

Monument
30 August 1969

Worth the climb

30 August 1969

The view from Monument, looking down Monument Street to the junction with
Lower Thames Street, with Billingsgate Market (centre right) and Custom House
beyond. Curiously, we often look upon familiar features as having always
occupied their particular spot on the map, yet in the case of Tower Bridge, it
wasn't opened until 1894.

Worth another climb

30 October 1969

The view from St Paul's Cathedral towards the south west and a still acceptable
face of London.

Not for the squeamish

30 October 1969

Don't look now if you can't stand frights from heights. It is another aspect of the view from St Paul's, and I can't help thinking of Rumania when I look at it.

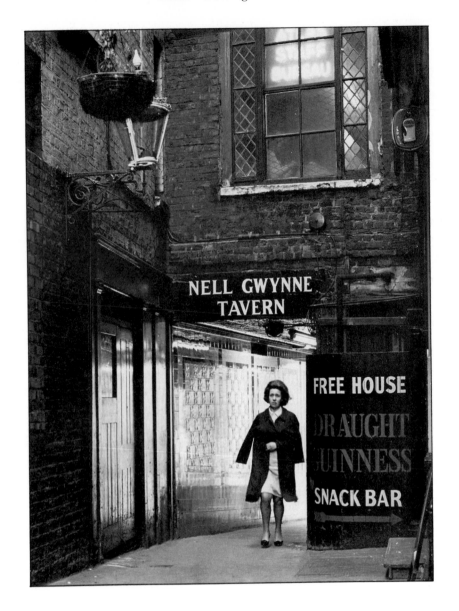

Sorrow-drowning, anyone?

29 October 1969

It's time we had some refreshment, though I can't for the life of me think where
the Nell Gwynne Tavern is. There's a girl in the window above, slaving away on
behalf of the Atlas Staff Bureau, but I don't expect she'll be able to help.

Shocking business in Regent Street . . .

31 October 1969

Winnie was in one heck of a fluff: 'Say, Fellas, he yelled, 'there's a coupla Limeys goggling at us thru' that there li'l ole winder.' 'Aw, Gee,' mumbled Eeyore, 'don't no one get no peace round heres no more?' Yes, folks, you got it in one: it's the Americanization of Pooh, and it ought to be a criminal offence. It's not merely shocking. It's tragic.

Superloo

Open Mondays to Saturdays 07 00 to 22 30   Sundays 09 00 to 22 00

Ladies' toilets, powder room, showers, bathrooms, toilet requisites.

Gentlemen's toilets, shaving facilities, showers, bathrooms, toilet requisites.

Entrance to facilities 1s (5p)

Includes use of toilet, soap, and towel

Use of shower (additional) 3s 6d (17½p)

Includes personal pack containing bath towel, soap, bath mat.

Use of bathroom (additional) 5s (25p)

Includes personal pack containing bath towel, soap, bath mat.

(Figures in brackets are the decimal equivalent prices.)

Standard toilet facilities are available opposite the left luggage
locker area adjoining platform 3.

Superlootives

8 April 1970

Didn't take British Rail long to get there with the fancy language and new
images, once they decided to turn Euston into a travel clinic instead of a railway
terminus.

Impressionism

Outside and returned to sanity, it was soothing to find super-soft snow caressing
the cheek, although the reduced visibility caused some difficulty in locating the
railway relics shop, known as 'Collectors' Corner'. It turned out to be through the
door, halfway up the wall at the top of the steps. They were carrying a sizeable
stock of tickets, railwaymen's watches, lamps, uniform caps, signalling equip-
ment and locomotive name- and number-plates on the day I went.

133

I'm forever blowing bubbles
8 April 1970

The light of the modern world. Later the same day, after the snow flurries had
dispersed.

Curtailed vision

28 August 1970

Fancy choosing a hazy day in August for a trip to the observation floor of the Shell
Building.

Excuse me, but can you direct me to the nearest desert?

28 August 1970

I have an idea we need look no further than the Hayward Gallery, Britain's Mecca
for pyramids.

Worrying statistic

28 August 1970

Is there no longer anything we can eat, drink, say, think or do, without killing or maiming ourselves? The latest bad news to emerge is that deckchairs injure 3,000 people a year in this country.

Lack of uplift

29 August 1970

Attempted kite-flying in Kensington Gardens. He wasted his time, got red in the face, drained his energy and exhausted his muscles. His spectating wife looked infinitely more at ease and – dare I suggest it? – safer.

Round Pond life at Kensington Gardens
29 August 1970

The bride looked a picture

29 August 1970

Hampstead annual open-air art exhibition.

And so did they

29 August 1970

Shadows with substance: a pair of framed silhouettes at Kenwood . . . But the
British public simply doesn't appreciate art.

Anachronism ahoy!
29 October 1971

And with a vengeance, for here is a reproduction of the fictitious eighteenth-century *Hispaniola*, built for the 1950 film version of *Treasure Island*, moored in the Thames, opposite the twentieth-century HMS *Belfast* (barely visible), upstream of the nineteenth-century Tower Bridge which was opened somewhere around the time of Robert Louis Stevenson's death. The stern-looking children are strictly twentieth century. The one on the right is the former Miss National Nature Week of 1963, and the other is Bridget, of slightly later vintage.

Leftist tendencies

25 March 1973

Both temptation and leaning are plainly present, but will it make the turn?
Hampstead Grove.

Straight and narrow
25 March 1973

Extremely narrow and made optically narrower by the double yellow lines. The carriageway is no more than four cat lengths in width, explaining the car's presence on the footpath. The Friends' Meeting House is most sensibly situated. Avoidance of anyone would seem a remote possibility at such a location. Hampstead.

Lost and found

2 November 1973

It's a familiar enough sight: lost boy, helpful passer-by and policemen, racking their brains to discover who he is and where he comes from. This Oxford Street episode is far-removed from the picture of police insensitivity presented nowadays. Incidentally, have you noticed the bus-change in the second photograph?

Small business survey

2 November 1973

I think this was in Regent Street, which doesn't automatically spring to mind as
the hub of the roast chestnut industry. The photographic evidence adds some
weight to the claim, by showing how three out of three customers emerging from
Barclay's Bank had no intention of buying any.

Buyers' Market

3 November 1973

Book buyers, that is. Always lively interest centred on the Farringdon Road
tables.

Washing day
3 November 1973

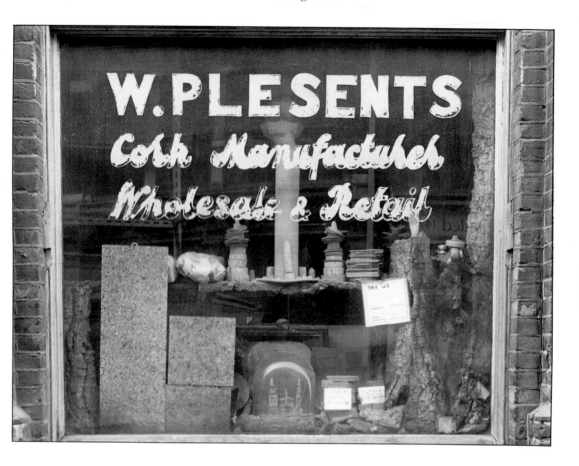

Cork display
3 November 1973

Matter in hand

3 November 1973

W. Plesents was London's last cork manufacturer, and on the point of closing down when we called on the proprietor, Mr Day, who treated us like valued old customers instead of total strangers, and insisted on carving a small sailing boat for each of the girls. And when he locked up the shop at Saturday lunchtime, he waved goodbye as if we were long lost friends.

Keep us postered. We're proud of our names
31 August 1974

A collection of commercials in Castlehaven Road.

Keep us out of it. We're strictly incognito

31 August 1974

Well, it is a great age for calling yourself something different or being someone else. The problem here is a vexing one: is Yvonne Darcy (who dances 'Like your mother wouldn't like it') really Yvonne Darcy, or has she changed her name to avoid recognition by her own mother?

Kentish Town clutter

31 August 1974

Not far from the underground station's entrance. The public house in the
background is The Assembly House. As for the foreground, it is more of a
disassembly, though with character.

Bomb warning

31 August 1974

The entrance to Goodge Street Station.

HUMANITY

EDITH CAVELL
BRUSSELS
DAWN
OCTOBER 12TH
1915
PATRIOTISM IS NOT ENOUGH
I MUST HAVE NO HATRED OR
BITTERNESS FOR ANYONE

Life extinguished

31 August 1974

The Edith Cavell Memorial in Charing Cross Road.

Still life with lamps
31 August 1974

What draws a crowd?
31 August 1974

A crowd, drawing a man
31 August 1974

Demand supplied

31 August 1974

Feeding an orderly queue of sparrows in St James's Park.

Supply disrupted

8 November 1974

Covent Garden Market, three days before its closure on 11 November 1974.

Shifting sacks

Searching sisters

Head-on meeting

Littered corner

Conversational corners
8 November 1974

These, and the other Covent Garden views, have been selected from a total of around 130, taken purely because I was lucky enough to be in London, though with little more than an hour to spare. It was 'last gasp' coverage, catching the subject in its death-throes.

Cat . . .
11 October 1975

. . . and mousetrap

11 October 1975

Still catching people, though now re-set at St Martin's Theatre instead of the
original Ambassadors.

Man exhausted

March 1976

And who wouldn't be, after a day's footslogging round the *Daily Mail* Ideal
Home Exhibition at Olympia. Exactly a week later, a bomb exploded there.

Of course they do!

1 January 1978

But they don't need to paint all over other people's walls in order to prove the
point.

Hunched over the headlines
11 October 1975

A newsvendor at Cambridge Circus.

Hoisted high above the tablets
1 January 1978

Karl Marx enjoys everlasting life in a democracy – for only in a true democracy is
the dissenter allowed to stand head and, er, shoulders above the crowd. Mr Marx
even had what seemed to be a self-appointed and permanent attendant to keep the
shrine neat and tidy.

Retiring collection
1 January 1978

Life's great closing time
1 January 1978

The show must go on
2 January 1978

A medley of musical posters at the corner of Drury Lane and Stukeley Street.

Just a couple of lines
2 January 1978

The couple of lines were in the window of Philip Poole & Co. Ltd., also in Drury Lane. As with a certain radio sketch, they too instantly imprinted themselves for ever:

> 'They come as a Boon and a Blessing to men,
> The Pickwick, the Owl and the Waverley Pen.'

Followed by a single column . . .

... bringing us neatly back to base, or square one.
3 June 1978

EPILOGUE

...would have been impossible to portray London's ...stness and diversity in so few pages and impres- ...ons. The photographs selected are no more than ...flections of my own likes and dislikes, and I can ...ly hope that the little curiosities and pieces of ...sual history which appealed to me at the time ...ill now have proved equally interesting to you. ...egrettably, for every item included, half a dozen ...ore have had to be left out.

After years of conditioning by humorists and ...mic characters like Denry Machin in Arnold ...ennett's 'The Card', of whom it was said in the ...osing lines, 'He's identified with the great cause ...cheering us all up', I'll be more than satisfied if ...have managed to retain your attention without ...ving offence.

M.D.